An Introduction to Coping with

Anxiety

2nd Edition

Contents

About This Book

Most of us feel anxious at certain times in our day-to-day lives – for instance when we feel scared or threatened by a situation and think that we may not be able to deal with it effectively. Taking an important exam, going to a job interview and making a public speech are some of the situations people often describe as anxiety-provoking. Usually, as the situation passes, the anxiety drops. While everyone feels anxious at times, for some of us anxiety can seem unbearable and unmanageable.

For some people, anxiety never seems to go away, even when the problems they face are minor, or would seem manageable to others. And a few experience such extreme anxiety that it begins to interfere with their daily lives and they feel they just can't cope any more. This can be confusing and frightening, and they may start to worry that it will never get any better.

This book will help you understand what's going on when you feel anxious. Part 1 describes the symptoms of anxiety and explains the way in which these are maintained in what becomes a vicious circle. Part 2 then gives you practical skills you can use to combat the symptoms of anxiety in three important areas – your physical symptoms, your thinking and your behaviour. By understanding and learning these key skills you can turn your problems with anxiety into things of the past.

It's often helpful to write things down, and Part 2 of the book describes several exercises that will help you cope with your anxiety on a day-to-day basis, with completed examples to guide you. It's a good idea to have a notebook handy when you begin to work through these, so that you can keep a record of your thoughts, feelings and progress, as suggested in the various exercises.

Good luck!

Brenda Hogan and Lee Brosan

Part 1: ABOUT ANXIETY

1

So What Is Anxiety?

Sitting an exam, going for a job interview, meeting future in-laws, having to make a complaint at your child's school – there are many situations that may make you feel anxious just by thinking about them, and dealing with the actual event can be a major ordeal. Worrying is usually a major part of anxiety, and for people who struggle with anxiety, it may feel uncontrollable. But worrying isn't the only problem! Anxiety affects the way we feel, both emotionally and physically, and the way we act. The following symptoms are common:

- feeling nervous, anxious or frightened

- feeling irritable or easily upset

- having difficulty concentrating or focusing

- heart beating faster (or heart 'flutters')

- shortness of breath

- sweating

- trembling

- tense muscles

- dry mouth

- feeling sick/stomach upset

- 'butterflies' in the stomach

- feeling light-headed

- difficulty sleeping

- a desire to avoid or escape the anxiety-provoking situation.

Feeling anxious can make life miserable. You can end up worrying too much, going over and over the worries in your mind, and finding it simpler just to avoid or leave situations that are likely to cause you anxiety.

Anxiety tends to affect your body (physical symptoms), the way you feel, the way you think, and the way you act. This can be a helpful way to think about anxiety, and we will discuss this more below.

Before we go on, however, let's start to demystify the experience of anxiety. The first step to overcoming anxiety is to understand anxiety and recognise it for what it is. Sometimes people have beliefs about anxiety that make it seem a lot worse, or more dangerous, than it really is. Understanding some of the basic facts about anxiety can be helpful.

Some Facts About Anxiety

1. Anxiety is normal. You would be hard-pressed to find anyone who has not experienced anxiety at some point! Anxiety is a normal and expected part of the human experience.

2. Anxiety is adaptive. This means that anxiety exists in order to help and protect us. Anxiety helps us deal with danger (e.g. to quickly jump out of the way of a speeding car) and to perform at our best (e.g. anxiety is what motivates us to prepare for important situations, such as a big presentation at work).

3. Anxiety is NOT dangerous. Anxiety does feel highly uncomfortable, but it is not dangerous. Remember, anxiety is there to help and protect us, not harm us.

4. Anxiety does not last for ever. Feelings of anxiety may increase at times, but they will always come down again. Anxiety may feel like it is going to last for ever, but it is temporary.

5. Anxiety is invisible. Worrying, as well as the emotional and physical feelings of anxiety, are things that happen on the inside. Even though it may feel like our anxiety is apparent to all around us, others do not usually know we are anxious unless we tell them.

6. Problems with anxiety are common. You are not alone!

Anxiety impacts us physically and emotionally, and affects the way we think and the way we behave. Understanding how anxiety works is an important part of making it more manageable.

How Does Anxiety Affect Your Body?

> I start getting hot and sweaty and my mouth gets really dry. My heart pounds in my chest. Sometimes I even find it hard to breathe. The worse I feel, the more I want to run away ...

You may have heard of the 'fight-or-flight' response. This is a physical response that occurs in alarming circumstances – your reaction will either be to fight in order to protect yourself or to run in order to escape the danger (another option is to 'freeze' in order to make yourself less noticeable). This is our bodies' safety mechanism designed to allow us to respond in an emergency. It is associated with many physical changes:

- breathing faster to increase oxygen in the body

- faster heart rate to increase blood flow to the muscles

- more tension in muscles for a quick response

- less saliva, causing a dry mouth

- trembling or shaking

- sweating to cool the body down

- mind focusing on the source of the threat.

These changes help us respond quickly and effectively to dangerous situations that require a physical response. For instance, increased blood and oxygen flow to the muscles makes us stronger and faster. This survival mechanism has evolved over millions of years to protect us from danger and can still be very useful to us today – we can act fast to jump out of the way of an oncoming vehicle or to run after a small child who is just about to walk in front of a swing in the park. Although these physical symptoms can be very uncomfortable (and very noticeable if you aren't busy running or fighting for your life!), they are not dangerous. Remember, they are protective, not harmful.

Here's the problem: modern life is rarely dangerous on a physical level. If you have an important presentation coming up at work or are about to go out on a first date, running away, fighting, or freezing up are not very helpful! While these kinds of responses do come in handy from time to time, many of today's anxiety-provoking situations do not require the fight-or-flight physical response. In these situations, it is more helpful to think in a productive, helpful way.

In some cases these physical changes are necessary and helpful, and can protect us from danger. In fact, having this kind of physical response can be helpful in almost any stressful situation because it alerts us that we need to attend to a situation, which can motivate us to act when we should (e.g. to start preparing for that important presentation). But as we have seen, it is often a mental response that is required rather than a physical one. The unused physical activity in your body can be very uncomfortable and even distressing, but it is important to remind yourself that the physical symptoms you are experiencing are normal and not dangerous.

How Does Anxiety Affect Your Feelings?

> Sometimes when I worry I feel really awful. My worries go round and round in circles in my head and I start to think that I won't be able to cope. The more I worry, the worse I feel – I feel anxious, on edge and tense. Sometimes it gets so bad that I can't sit still.

Anxiety is a mixture of emotions, from feeling nervous, 'stressed', and on edge, to panicky or frightened. A certain level of anxiety is normal – everyone has these moments – and even useful, as it makes us pay attention to situations that may be dangerous. If our ancient ancestors hadn't felt anxious about coming face-to-face with a sabre-toothed tiger, they might have walked straight into its jaws. In modern life, the feelings of anxiety still keep us safe – for example, feeling nervous as you stand at the edge of a cliff makes it more likely that you will take a step back and less likely that you will fall off. Or you might feel anxious about walking home late at night along a dark alley, so you take the well-lit, perhaps longer, route instead – this is good sense and means you are less likely to be mugged. Even in less dangerous situations, the feelings of anxiety can prompt us to take action in a productive way – it can motivate you to work extra hard on that presentation for your boss, or to allow extra time so you are not late when you drop your kids off at school.

So some anxiety is normal and necessary, even though we don't enjoy the sensation. It helps us avoid potentially dangerous or harmful situations. However, feelings of anxiety become problematic when they are in excess of what would be expected given the situation, or if they stay with you most of the time. Another concern is the emotions that are secondary to persistent anxiety, such as feeling irritable or easily upset.

How Does Anxiety Affect Your Thoughts?

> When I hear a rattle in the car I start worrying right away. I can't sleep because I'm thinking about what might be wrong and I'm worried about how much it will cost.

The way we think about things is an important part of anxiety. As you've seen earlier, one part of the flight-or-fight response was 'mind focusing on the source of threat'. When you're in real danger, it's clearly sensible to focus on the source of the threat – you wouldn't want to ignore a car hurtling towards you as you cross the road! But some people react in the same way to situations which are not at all threatening or dangerous, or they overestimate the true level of danger. When this happens, their bodies go into fight-or-flight mode, and they feel anxious even when the situation is relatively safe.

Some people are constantly on the lookout for possible sources of danger, which increases their anxiety. They may worry that things will go wrong even when there is no reason to believe that this will happen – like worrying that the alarm won't go off even though it has never failed before, or worrying that a family member driving a long distance might get in a car accident even though that person has a clean driving record and drives long distances quite frequently – this kind of thinking almost always leads to feelings of anxiety.

The kind of thinking that leads to anxiety is called 'worrying'. Worrying and anxiety are very closely linked; the more worried you are and the more frequently you worry, the more anxious you will feel. So what exactly is worrying?

Worrying involves thinking about negative events that might happen in the future. It often involves 'what if…?' scenarios:

What if I am late for work?
What if I fail my exam?
What if we spend too much money while we are
    on holiday?
What if my child gets bullied at school?

People tend to worry about the same sorts of things. Even those who struggle with high anxiety seem to worry about similar things that others worry about. Common worry topics include minor day-to-day problems, problems at work or school, the health and/or safety of loves ones or themselves, issues related to family and close friends, and issues related to the world (e.g. safety, stability or the environment) or the future. The difference between those who struggle with anxiety and those who do not tends to be *how much* they worry about these things.

One thought leads to another … and another … and another …

You may find that when you start worrying, you start off with a relatively minor concerning thought, but that quickly leads to a chain of other worries. Sometimes each successive worry is worse than the last.

For example, you might start off by thinking:

'My boss didn't even say hello to me this morning. I wonder if she is upset with me?'

This might lead to other worries, such as:

'What if she is upset that I asked to leave early yesterday to take my son to the doctor?'

'Maybe she is not happy with the work I have done so far on this project?'

And these worries, in turn, may lead to even more catastrophic thoughts, such as:

What if I get fired?

What if I can't find another job?

Will we be able to pay the mortgage? What if we lose our house?

This kind of thought process is known as chaining – one thought leads to many others, with a tendency for thoughts to successively become more dramatic and stressful.

Some people feel that worry and anxiety are interfering with their lives. When this happens, people often complain that they 'worry all the time'. They feel as though their worrying is out of control. It's hardly a surprise that all this worrying increases their feelings of anxiety.

How Does Anxiety Affect Your Behaviour?

> I used to really like having friends over for a meal. But then I started getting worried about getting everything 'just right' … I would spend days planning the food and cleaning the house, and I would worry so much that it spoiled the fun. After our friends left I would worry about whether they had really had a good time. So I just stopped having people over.

> I used to like travelling and going to new places, but now I'm too scared to go far away from home.

So anxiety can change how we lead our lives.

There are two major ways that anxiety can affect our behaviour – and both of them are attempts to reduce anxiety. The first is avoidance, and the second is safety behaviours. Many people avoid situations that make them anxious. If they know that a situation might cause them to worry and feel anxious, they just stay away from it. They may stop going to parties where they don't know many people, or they go but leave early if they begin to feel nervous. Other people use 'safety behaviours' – for example they may stay close to a friend or family member or always offer to help in the kitchen when faced with a social situation that makes them feel anxious. Or they may keep a 'safety object' with them, such as a bottle of water in case their mouth gets dry, or their mobile phone that they can use to 'look busy' if they are feeling anxious about talking to others in the room.

Avoiding situations that make you anxious and using safety behaviours are common – and they work, but *only in the short term*. In the long term, people find it even more difficult to deal with their anxieties because this way of behaving gives you false messages, such as 'the only reason nothing terrible happened is because I didn't go' or 'the only reason I coped was because I sat in the kitchen all night' or 'I got out just in time'.

Avoidance and safety behaviours lead to more anxiety and make it more difficult to face similar situations in the future. Also, your list of safety behaviours and avoided situations grows longer and longer – which can start to really impact your life and what you are able to do.

Anxiety can affect our behaviour in other ways as well. Often, people who struggle with anxiety have a hard time dealing with situations in which they feel uncertain: for example, uncertain about what they should do, or uncertain about what is going to happen, or uncertain as to whether they are making the right decision. To help deal with this they often engage in behaviours that they hope will make them feel more certain. Some examples of this include:

- Reassurance seeking – this can involve asking repeatedly for others opinions.

- Asking others to make decisions – this is actually a form of avoidance, since it avoids the possibility that you might not make the 'right' choice.

- Checking – for example, calling a loved one's mobile phone repeatedly to make sure they are all right, or checking their work repeatedly for errors.

- Excessive preparation – making very long to-do lists, or performing excessive research before making a decision.

Just like other forms of avoidance and safety behaviours, these strategies do not work in the long term and actually serve to keep anxiety going.

2

Anxiety's Vicious Circle

Unfortunately, the different aspects of anxiety – emotional, physical, thoughts and behaviour – work together to form a vicious circle of anxiety. First, for example, let's imagine that you are about to give some sort of presentation at work but you're worried about speaking in public. Second, thinking about the presentation makes you nervous, which triggers the fight-or-flight response, so you feel short of breath and shaky. Third, you'll probably think that everyone will now see how nervous you are and they'll know you're not up to it. This, of course, will increase your nervousness. Fourth, the physical response will then get stronger, which will make you worry even more, producing a vicious circle like the one below.

ANXIOUS THOUGHT
(They'll think
I'm no good)

PHYSICAL RESPONSE
(Breathless, shaky)

Many treatments of anxiety are now based on a successful method known as cognitive behavioural therapy (CBT). This method teaches you how certain ways of thinking are actually causing the anxiety by giving you a distorted picture of what's going on in your life, and helps you weaken the connections between the situations that worry you and your anxious reaction to them. CBT suggests that it is the first part of this vicious circle (the anxious thought) that is most important in producing anxiety. If you tend to see things as threatening and dangerous, and imagine that the worst will happen, then you are very likely to feel anxious.

When you are feeling anxious you may be affected by all four parts of the vicious circle (physical responses, emotions, thoughts and behaviours), or you may only notice problems with one or two. To work out what causes the most problems for you, ask yourself the questions below.

Physical symptoms

Do I suffer from any of these symptoms: racing heart, shortness of breath, light-headedness, 'butterflies' in my stomach, trembling or dry mouth?

Emotions

Do I often feel anxious, nervous, or edgy?

Thoughts

Is worrying a problem for me? Do I feel that my worrying is out of control? Do I worry about 'anything and everything'?

Behaviour

Do I avoid doing certain things because they make me feel nervous or worried?

If I start to feel nervous in a particular situation, do I try to escape as quickly as I can?

Do I avoid doing things by myself because I feel more comfortable when someone else is with me?

Do I use 'tricks' to try to feel less anxious or to disguise the fact that I am anxious (for example, making sure I stay close to someone I know, avoiding eye contact or playing with my mobile phone)?

Although it may seem impossible to change how you feel, it can be done! Because all four parts of anxiety work together, if you work on changing one area, it will help with the others too. So by making changes to how you think or behave, or to how your body reacts, you can make big changes to how you *feel*. In Part 2 of this book we show you how to do this.

Part 2: COPING WITH ANXIETY

Anxiety is a normal part of being human. As we have discussed, in many situations it is adaptive, or helpful, for us to experience anxiety – it can keep us out of harm's way and can motivate us to take action. It is important to remember that coping with anxiety does not involved getting rid of anxiety completely. Rather, your goal should be to better manage your anxiety so that you can live a calmer, happier life.

It may be helpful to think about your anxiety response like an overly sensitive smoke alarm. You do not want to get rid of the smoke alarm in your home as that would be dangerous. Rather, you want to make sure your smoke alarm only goes off when it is necessary – not when you burn the toast! The same holds true for anxiety. You do not want to get rid of anxiety. It is there for a reason – you need it, but not all the time. You want to make sure that you are not experiencing anxiety in response to situations that don't warrant it.

3

Calming Your Body Down: Managing the Physical Symptoms of Anxiety

Most of us find the physical symptoms we described in Part 1 unpleasant and difficult to cope with. The following exercises are specifically designed to help reduce the feelings caused by anxiety. This is a great place to start – if you can slow down the physical response to anxiety, you will be in a better place to use some of the other strategies we will talk about later in this book.

Over-breathing

You've probably noticed that your breathing becomes shallower and faster when you are very anxious – this is called 'over-breathing'. Sometimes this will be very obvious, but some people don't realise that their breathing has changed. It's not dangerous to breathe more quickly and shallowly – it's similar to the way you breathe when exercising – but if you breathe like this when you are not exercising, you may have some uncomfortable side-effects, such as dizziness or feeling 'faint', tingling in the hands or feet, and your vision may seem distorted. Oddly enough, one side-effect of over-breathing is that it can make you feel as if you're not getting enough air. Trying to breathe more will actually make the symptoms worse, not better. Again, it is not dangerous to breathe more, but it will result in temporary discomfort.

A good way to counteract the symptoms of incorrect breathing and to reduce the physical symptoms of anxiety is to use the Controlled Breathing technique described.

Controlled Breathing

When you first try this exercise, lie down, or sit in a comfortable chair. As you become more experienced with controlled breathing, you can try it sitting upright or standing.

1. Place one hand on your chest and the other on your stomach.

2. Breathe in deeply and slowly through your nose, allowing your tummy and chest to swell gently. Look down at your hands. Is your lower hand moving? Good. This

means that you are using all your lung space, not just panting from the top of your lungs. Ideally, you should see gentle movement in both your top and lower hands. If not, try to push your tummy out very slightly as you breathe in. This will encourage breathing from the whole of your lungs.

3. The in-breath should be slow, gentle and quiet – no one else should be able to hear you breathe.

4. Hold the breath briefly.

5. Breathe out, slowly and gently.

6. After breathing out, pause for a moment. Don't take the next breath in until you feel it is 'time'.

7. Repeat this process. Try to get a rhythm going. Keep the breathing slow, deep and gentle.

Tense Muscles

Relaxation techniques can help you calm down and lower your overall level of anxiety. Below, you'll find a set of instructions for progressive muscle relaxation. Read them through a couple of times before starting. (You might find it easier to record the instructions onto your phone so you can play it while trying the technique.) Try the exercise at least twice a day at first and allow yourself about thirty minutes (it probably won't take that long, but you don't want to feel rushed, so allow yourself a bit of extra time). Choose a time when you are alone and not expecting interruptions; and remember to switch off your mobile! Sit or lie down in a comfortable place. It helps if the room is restful, warm and pleasantly lit. Try not to worry about whether you are 'doing it right'. The most important thing is to give it a try. Remember that relaxation will not work if you read about it but don't give it a try. The more you do it, the better you will get.

Progressive Muscle Relaxation

1. Find a comfortable position with your arms resting loosely at your sides, legs uncrossed. Be still for a few minutes to help you get into the right frame of mind and allow yourself to start to unwind. Take a couple of deep breaths. Focus on your breathing, and let your muscles slowly relax.

2. If you feel uncomfortable, change your position at any time – you don't have to

worry about staying completely still. If your mind wanders during the exercise, bring your attention back to your breathing.

3. Now roll your neck gently from side to side to loosen your muscles. Raise your shoulders up to your ears, hold them there, and then drop your shoulders. Let the weight of your shoulders fall gently back down. Focus on your breathing. Breathe slowly and gently, in through your nose, and out through your mouth. Let yourself relax. Imagine that each time you breathe out, you let go of some of the tension.

4. Now turn all your attention to your feet and how they feel. Tighten the muscles by raising your feet up a little bit, and pointing your toes towards the ceiling. Feel the tension in your feet, toes and calves. Notice the tension and tightness in the muscles. Hold this for about five seconds and then let it go. Relax. Let the tension melt away to be replaced by a wave of relaxation. Concentrate on the changing sensations in your muscles as they move from a tense state to a more relaxed one. Relax your feet and toes. Focus on how that feels, as you gently breathe in and out. Focus on the feeling of relaxation for about twenty seconds.

5. Now tighten the hip and leg muscles by pressing down on your heels. You should feel tension in your calves and in your upper legs. Focus on that tension and the tightness. Hold it for about five seconds, and then relax. Feel the tension draining out of your legs, being replaced by a comfortable feeling of relaxation. Imagine the muscles smoothing out, becoming soft and relaxed. Focus on the relaxation for about twenty seconds as the tension just slips away.

6. Now for your abdomen. Tighten your tummy muscles as much as you can. Suck in your tummy and hold the tension. Focus on the tightness and tension for about five seconds. Then relax – allow the muscles to go limp and loose. Let the relaxed sensation spread slowly and gently over your abdomen. Keep your attention on the feelings of calm relaxation for about twenty seconds.

7. The next step focuses on your chest muscles. Take a deep breath in through your nose. Hold it. Feel the tension around your rib cage. Hold it for a moment, and then let it go. Breathe out gently and slowly. Feel the changes in your chest as you breathe out.

8. Breathe in deeply, filling your lungs, hold it, notice the tension, and then release it, breathing out through your mouth. Let your chest muscles relax. Return to slow and gentle breathing. Focus on the feeling of relaxation.

9. Now turn your attention to your hands and forearms. Place your hands palm up. Squeeze them into fists as tightly as you can, and turn the fists towards the ceiling. Feel the tension in your fingers, palms and forearms for about five seconds, and then let go. Slowly and gently, let your hands and arms relax. Let the relaxation spread over your arms, hands and fingers as the tension drains away. Remember to focus on the relaxed feeling for about twenty seconds.

10. Now for the rest of your arms. Create tension by pressing your hands down as hard as you can and feel the tightness and tension. Hold it for about five seconds, then let it go. Let your hands rest gently and comfortably. Allow the tension to slip away. Focus on the relaxation in your arms for about twenty seconds.

11. And now try to tense all the muscles in your neck for about five seconds, then shoulder muscles. Focus on the feeling of relaxation for about twenty seconds.

12. Now take a moment to focus on your shoulders. Notice any tension already there. Then tense the muscles by shrugging. Pull your shoulders up towards your ears, as if there was a string pulling them up. Hold the position for five seconds, noticing the tightness and tension. Then slowly relax, letting your shoulders gently drop back down. Focus on relaxing the muscles in your shoulders. Focus on this feeling of relaxation for about twenty seconds.

13. Move your attention to your mouth and jaw. Tense this area by clenching your teeth and pulling your mouth into a forced smile. Your lips, cheeks and jaw should feel very tense and tight. Hold it for about five seconds and then relax your face. Feel the muscles loosen and become soft. Allow your teeth to part and the muscles to soften and relax. Let the relaxation spread across your jaw and mouth. Remember to focus on the feeling of relaxation for about twenty seconds.

14. Now move up to your eyes and nose. Close your eyes as tightly as you can, and wrinkle your nose. Feel the tension in your face, your upper cheeks and eyes. Focus on the tension for five seconds. And then relax. Notice the tension slipping away. Imagine your muscles becoming smooth and relaxed. Focus on the feeling of relaxation for about twenty seconds.

15. You have now reached your forehead. Raise your eyebrows as high as you can. Notice the tension and tightness in your forehead and scalp. Hold it for five seconds then let go. Feel the relaxation spread back from your forehead, all the way across your scalp, for twenty seconds.

16. You have now gone through all the muscle groups in your body. Continue to relax, and each time you breathe out, allow yourself to become even more relaxed. Each time you breathe out, think of a part of your body, and then allow the muscles to relax even more.

17. When you have completed the relaxation exercise, take a moment to let yourself become more alert. Open your eyes, and move your arms and legs around a little bit before you get up and start being active again.

When you first try this exercise, you may find it difficult to relax your muscles, or you may have trouble concentrating on relaxing. That's why it is important to practise the techniques – it takes time and practice to be able to relax effectively. If you practise twice a day, you'll start to notice that it takes you a shorter time to relax. When you feel ready, reduce the amount of time you spend practising and use your skills whenever you feel you need them. With practice, you'll become more aware when your muscles are tense, and will be able to relax them 'on-the-spot'. Use this technique whenever you feel yourself getting nervous.

Too Much Caffeine

Your body reacts to caffeine in much the same way as it reacts during the fight-or-flight response. So too much caffeine will make your anxiety feel much worse.

Caffeine is in coffee, tea (including green tea and some flavoured teas), cola (and some other fizzy drinks – check the ingredients list to be sure) and chocolate.

Think about how much of each of these items you consume daily. It's probably more than you think, so might want to keep a 'caffeine diary' for a few days to keep track.

Caffeine is addictive, so the more you have the more you become dependent on it. Your tolerance of it will increase – you'll need more caffeine to get the same effects – and you'll experience withdrawal symptoms if you don't get it. Common withdrawal symptoms include headaches, tiredness and shakiness, as well as a strong urge to have a cup of coffee or tea! So if you are drinking a lot of caffeine, you may find it quite difficult to go 'cold turkey' and stop having it. To avoid the unpleasant withdrawal symptoms, reduce the amount of caffeine you drink gradually. The good news is that you don't have to cut it from your diet completely. Small amounts of caffeine – a cup of coffee or tea in the morning – do not have a major impact on anxiety levels. Decaffeinated drinks are a good alternative.

Cut caffeine out completely in the late afternoons and evenings if you're having problems sleeping.

4

Don't Worry So Much! Learning to Manage Anxious Thoughts

Generally, when we talk about 'anxiety' we mean the whole picture – thinking, feeling, physical changes and behaviour. When we talk about 'worry' we are referring to the thinking part of anxiety. Worrying is a very big part of the problem for people who struggle with anxiety. Worrying almost always leads to high levels of all the other parts of anxiety. Anxiety can also lead to more worrying – you've probably noticed that when you are anxious, you think about things in a very different way from when you are relaxed. Things that normally wouldn't worry you may seem like total disasters. You may find yourself thinking that 'everything will go wrong' or that you will be unable to cope. You may even find yourself worrying about things that never bothered you before, like why your partner is ten minutes late back from work – has he or she been involved in an accident? Or is that cough you have really a sign of a serious disease?

People struggling with worrying and anxiety are likely to think about things in very extreme terms. For example, they probably believe:

- It is *very likely* that things will go wrong.

- When things do go wrong, they will go *dreadfully wrong*.

- When things do go wrong, they will be *unable to cope*.

This way of thinking is likely to make anxiety even worse. People who 'get stuck' in these thought patterns find themselves in a vicious circle. The more you worry, the more anxious you feel. And the more anxious you feel, the more you worry.

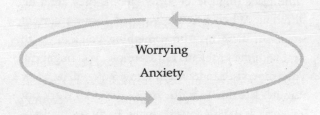

Worrying

Anxiety

The trick here is to break the circular link between worrying and anxiety. Although this sounds difficult, you can learn to change the way you think, and see things in a way that is much less likely to make you feel anxious.

People who are struggling with worrying tend to worry about either current problems or hypothetical situations. Current problems include things that are happening right now in your life – for example, 'This traffic is terrible! I think I'm going to be late for work', or 'We spent too much money this month. I'm worried that we won't be able to pay the bills'. Hypothetical situations are situations that may (or may not) occur at some point in the future. Examples of hypothetical situations that you might worry about are, 'What if my daughter doesn't get into university?', or 'What if mortgage rates go up and we can't afford this house any more?'

Although these two types of worrying lead to the same place (high levels of anxiety!), they are a bit different. When you are worried about a current situation, there may be something you can do to deal with the problem. For example, you might call your supervisor to let them know you will be a few minutes late due to traffic, or sit down to work out a plan to deal with your finances. In these situations, you have some degree of control. A good coping strategy involves replacing worrying with problem-solving. However, when you are worried about a hypothetical situation, you may have very little control and there may be no immediate problem-solving to do. For example, you personally have no control over mortgage rates, and there may be little you can do right now to ensure your six-year-old will eventually get into university. In these cases, the goal may be to manage the anxiety by learning to better tolerate uncertainty, rethink your worries, and work to reduce the amount of worrying that you do.

Before you start to work on reducing your amount of worrying, you need to identify and recognise your worries. Are you worried about current problems? About hypothetical situations? Are you imagining or focusing on possible terrible outcomes? Do you believe these outcomes are likely? Are you worried about your ability to cope? Figuring out what you are worrying about is the first step to managing worrying.

What Are You Worried About? Identifying Anxious Thoughts

Before you start to work on reducing worrying, you will need to recognise when you are worrying and work out which thoughts are making you anxious. This can be difficult as you may have become so used to worrying, and the thoughts may be so quick and automatic, that you don't even notice you are having them! So whenever you start feeling anxious, pay very close attention to what is going through your mind at that moment.

You may have thoughts such as 'I can't cope' or 'What if I screw up?' or you may have mental pictures, such as an image of a car accident or yourself doing something embarrassing. Both kinds of thoughts can cause high levels of anxiety.

Keeping a 'thought record' of situations that make you feel anxious and what you're thinking when you feel your anxiety rising can be a useful tool. To do this, first write down what you were doing when you started to feel anxious. Then ask yourself what you were thinking about when you started to feel anxious. (If it was an image, describe it.)

Finally, write down how you felt – your emotions. Anxiety isn't the only possibility. For example, you might also feel nervous, panicky or impatient.

Here is an example of a thought record.

Situation	What was I thinking about?	How did this make me feel?
Friend cancels lunch plans	Why did she cancel? Maybe she is angry with me.	Worried, anxious
Meeting at work	My work isn't good enough. Everyone will think I'm useless. What if I get the sack?	Anxious, panicky

Tip

Sometimes anxious thoughts are like 'flashes' and happen very quickly – without you paying much attention. For this reason, it's best to think about anxious thoughts when you are anxious. If you wait until you have calmed down, you may not be able to remember exactly what you were thinking.

In a notebook, or on a piece of paper, copy the headings in the example above and use this form to keep track of anxiety-provoking situations, your thoughts and your emotions. You might find it helpful to do this for a week or two in order to get a good sampling of the content of your worries. After this time, review your thought record. What do you notice?

- Are your thoughts 'extreme' – are you worried about potentially awful outcomes?

- Are you worried that these awful outcomes are likely to happen?

- Do you notice any 'chaining' – when one worry leads to another, and another, and so on?

- Are you worried about your ability to cope?

- Are you worried about current problems or hypothetical situations? Or both?

Sometimes people with anxiety are worried that paying attention to their worries may just make their anxiety worse. Remember, the worries are already there and you are already paying attention to them! The goal is to pay attention to your worries in a way that will be helpful instead of making it worse.

Strategies to Help Manage Worrying and Anxious Thoughts

There are multiple ways you can start to work on better managing – and ultimately reducing – your anxious thoughts. The following sections will cover several different strategies you can try to help cope with worrying. Some of these strategies may be more or less useful depending on the kind of worrying you are doing (this is discussed in more detail below). The goal is to help you develop a toolbox of strategies you can use to help you manage problematic worrying.

Challenging the thoughts that make you anxious

Have another look at your anxious thought record. Do you notice any signs of 'extreme' thinking – worrying about potentially horrible outcomes to situations? Do you find yourself thinking that these horrible outcomes are quite likely? Do you worry about your ability to cope? One way to help with this kind of worrying is to carefully evaluate whether this is really the most realistic way to think about things, or whether there is a more balanced alternative. Worrying thoughts are very often biased and based on guesses and exaggerations, rather than on facts. Learning how to think about the same situation in a more balanced way can help you break the vicious circle of anxiety so that you feel less anxious and better able to cope with difficulties. This kind of strategy can be useful for both current problems and hypothetical situations you are worried about.

At first it won't be easy to challenge your worrying thoughts. The technique of thought challenging (see below) is a tried and tested way to help you do this. This can be difficult at first, but the more you practise this, the easier and more 'natural' it will become.

To develop a more confident way of thinking, ask yourself these five questions:

- Are there any good reasons to be so worried?

- Are there any good reasons not to be so worried?

- Is there another way of looking at this?

- What is the worst that could happen?

- What can I do about it?

We discuss each of these questions in more detail below.

Are there any good reasons to be so worried?

When answering this question, ask yourself:

- What are the facts of the situation?

- Do the facts support what I think or do they contradict it?

- Would somebody else think my thoughts were based on facts?

Are there any good reasons not to be so worried?

Now ask yourself if there are any possible reasons why you should not be having this thought. Your answers to the first questions might give you some clues about why you don't need to be so worried. Another way to do this is to think of things that happened in the past that contradict your current worry. Or try to remember times when you worried about something similar and were wrong. You can also try asking yourself these questions:

• Am I jumping to conclusions?

• Am I predicting the future?

• Am I guessing what other people think?

• Am I overestimating the probability of this happening?

• Will this problem matter in one week/one month/one year from now?

Is there another way to look at this?

Whatever you are worrying about there is almost always another, more helpful way of looking at the problem. But when you're anxious it can seem impossible to see the wood for the trees. Another person's point of view may be helpful here – so ask yourself what someone else, perhaps a close friend you admire, might think in your situation. Alternatively, consider what you would say to a friend in a similar situation.

The alternative thoughts you come up with have to be realistic – if they're not, you simply won't believe them. You should think carefully about the alternate viewpoint in order to decide whether it is more realistic and helpful than the original thought worrying you.

What is the worst that could happen?

Anyone struggling with anxiety probably thinks about bad things happening in the future. These thoughts can be very disturbing, so you push them out of your mind without thinking things through carefully. But you need to confront these thoughts and ask yourself, 'What is the worst that could happen?' This may show that:

- Your worst fear is so exaggerated that it is extremely unlikely or even impossible.

- What you fear may be much less likely to happen than you previously predicted.

- Even if what you fear does happen, you may be able to cope with it better than you originally thought.

Once you've worked out what your worst fear is, ask yourself: 'How likely is it that this would actually happen?' This may be all you need to put the thought into perspective. It can be even more helpful to take it a stage further and ask yourself: 'How would I cope if this did happen?' Don't underestimate yourself. You probably have past experiences and personal skills that would help you cope in difficult situations (see below).

What can I do about it?

Ask yourself:

- Have I dealt with similar situations or with other stressful situations in the past? What did I do then that could help me now?

- What skills or abilities do I have that might help me cope with the situation?

- What advice would I give a friend who was in a similar situation?

- Who can I turn to for help, support or advice?

- Do I have all the facts I need? If not, how could I find out more?

You need to ask yourself what you can do in the immediate future to deal with the situation, and work out a specific plan. If you think you might benefit from some help with problem-solving, have a look at that section in this book (see pages 72–5).

Below is an example of the way thought challenging works.

In your notebook, copy the five questions below and use them to practise identifying and challenging your anxious thoughts. Remember, the more you practise, the easier it will get.

Thought challenging in action

Anxious thought: 'I have to present the results of the project I've been working on. My supervisor will be critical and disappointed in my work.'

Are there any good reasons to be so worried? My supervisor has been critical before, but she is critical of everyone.

Are there any good reasons not to be so worried? I worked hard on the project and finished it on time. I did a pretty good job. I worried about a similar situation a few months ago and everything turned out fine. My supervisor has praised my work in the past. My colleagues have said that I work hard and that I do a good job. I think that I may be overestimating the chances of my supervisor being critical.

Is there another way of looking at this? Maybe my supervisor will be satisfied with the report. Even if she has some criticisms, it won't mean that the entire report was a failure.

What is the worst that could happen? She may think the report is rubbish and I will lose my job. Realistically, I think it is very unlikely that I will lose my job over this. It is unrealistic that she will think the report is rubbish. If I did get fired, I would look for a new job. I have lots of experience, so it shouldn't be too difficult to find one fairly quickly.

What can I do about it? The report is done now, so there isn't much to do but wait. If my supervisor is critical, I will make some changes to the report. It will be important to think about her criticism rationally and not blow it out of proportion. It may also be a good idea to talk to my colleague Sally if I feel stressed so that I can get her perspective.

Rethinking what you believe about worry

For some people, it is not the content of their worries that is the problem. Thought challenging may help somewhat, but they find that when they get rid of one worry, another quickly takes it place. For people who struggle with worrying, it is often what they believe about worrying that is driving the problem. Some people believe that worrying serves a useful purpose – for example, they may believe that worrying helps them to be prepared, it motivates them, it prevents them from feeling upset or disappointed in the future, or it prevents negative outcomes. If someone believes that worrying has some sort of benefit, it can be very hard to stop! Other people believe that worrying is uncontrollable or harmful in some way. This tends to lead to 'worrying about worrying', which becomes a problem unto itself.

A very important part of managing anxiety and worrying is to recognise whether you hold any of these beliefs about worrying – and if you do, to rethink these beliefs in light of the facts about anxiety.

Challenging positive beliefs about worry

Most people who experience troublesome anxiety easily recognise that they worry too much. However, sometimes people may believe that there might be good things about worrying – we call these positive beliefs about worrying. For example, you might believe that worrying helps prepare you for problems, or that it protects you from experiencing negative emotions down the road, or even that it 'protects' you in some way from bad things happening. Positive beliefs about worrying may be hard to recognise. In fact, most people who do believe that worrying is useful or has some beneficial purpose don't even realise they hold these beliefs – until they take a closer look.

If you hold positive beliefs about worrying, it will very difficult to reduce or stop worrying. This makes sense, if you think about it. Why would you want to give up worrying if it serves some sort of useful purpose? It is therefore very important to identify positive beliefs about worrying – if you do hold these and don't do anything to change them, it will be hard to stop worrying.

Common positive beliefs about worrying are:

- Worrying helps me solve problems.

- Worrying helps me cope.

- If I worry, I can prevent bad things from happening.

- If I worry, I won't tempt fate.

- If I worry, I will be prepared.

- Worrying can prevent me from experiencing negative emotions in the future.

- Worrying means that I am a caring person.

Ask yourself: Are there any reasons why I shouldn't give up worrying completely? What are the reasons? What might happen if I do stop worrying?'

Write down your answers in your notebook.

Remember: these beliefs can convince you that you should be worrying. And, not surprisingly, this can lead to you worrying even more. It is very important to consider whether you think about worrying in a positive way, and if so, to weigh up the evidence for and against these beliefs. In the next section we show you how to do this.

We're now going to suggest how you can examine your thoughts about the positive effects of worrying and develop a fairer and more realistic way of thinking about the usefulness (or uselessness!) of worrying.

The advantages and disadvantages of worrying

Start by weighing up the advantages and disadvantages of worrying. There are a few examples of how you might do this in the box below.

Advantages of worrying	Disadvantages of worrying
Worrying helps me cope.	Worry makes me anxious and miserable. I don't think I really solve problems by worrying. When I get really anxious I'm worse at solving problems.
If I worry it will help me prepare in case the problem really happens.	I spend too much time worrying – it's a waste. Most of the time the things I worry about don't happen. Worry probably isn't helping me prepare – I think I would handle the problem in almost the same way if I didn't spend any time worrying beforehand.
Worrying protects me from experiencing negative emotions in the future.	Worrying causes me to feel terrible – it creates a negative emotion. I would probably be upset if something terrible happens, even if I worried about it beforehand.

Now try filling in a chart like this for yourself. Just thinking about and listing the pros and cons like this can help you realise just how many disadvantages there are to worrying.

Weighing up the evidence

Focusing on why you hold certain beliefs about the positive effects of worrying can be a useful exercise. Ask yourself the following questions:

- Do I have any evidence for my belief?

- If so, could there be an alternative explanation?

- Do I have any evidence against my belief?

- Would I be able to handle a bad situation if I had not worried about it beforehand?

- When I am worrying, am I really problem-solving? Or am I just going over the same thoughts again and again, without finding a solution?

- Can I think of any times in my life when I did not worry and events turned out positively?

• Does worrying really prevent bad things from happening, or make good things more likely? Or will good and bad things just happen, regardless of whether or not I worry?

• Does worrying really help me to cope, or does it interfere with my coping?

• What are the real effects of worrying – how is it affecting my life?

• How often does my worry really reflect reality? How often do I overestimate the likelihood of something going wrong?

• How often is my worrying really 'worth it'?

• If I stopped worrying, would it really mean I didn't care?

• Do I know any caring people who don't seem to worry as much as I do?

• Is there anything besides worrying that shows that I care?

• If something bad were to happen, would I really not be as upset because I had worried beforehand?

• Has anything bad ever happened in my life, even though I worried about it?

Use the previous questions in the following exercise. Remember that you need to consider the evidence for and against your positive belief about worrying.

On a new page in your notebook, write the heading:

What are my beliefs or thoughts about the positive effects or usefulness of worrying?

Then write down your belief or thought.

Under this, write two new column headings: 'Proof that this belief is correct' and 'Proof that this belief is incorrect'.

Under each heading, list the evidence for and against your belief. Use the questions on pages 54–5 to help guide you.

You have now considered the advantages and disadvantages of worrying, and weighed the evidence for and against your belief(s) about the positive effects of worrying. Based on all this information, you should be able to come up with a new, more realistic thought or belief about the effects of worrying. For example, a belief that 'If I worry, I will be more prepared' could be replaced with 'Worrying doesn't really help me prepare to deal with problems – it just makes me anxious and I feel terrible. I can deal with problems, whether I worry or not.'

Now write down in your notebook your own alternative, more realistic belief about the effect of worrying.

Remind yourself of this new belief whenever you find yourself worrying. This will take practice! You will probably notice you need to keep reminding yourself about this. Changing a belief that you may have held for a long time takes practice, but it can be done.

Evaluating 'old' versus 'new' beliefs about worrying

So now you have a 'new', more helpful and rational belief (or beliefs) about worrying to replace your 'old' belief about worrying. In order to further convince yourself that your 'new' belief about worrying is accurate and helpful, you may want to try a few experiments to help you to evaluate these beliefs.

Try the exercises below to help you weigh up your old and new belief(s) about the effects of worrying.

Evaluating old beliefs

Think of a time when you worried about an approaching event, such as attending a party or going to an unfamiliar place. Now describe the anxious thoughts that you had in as much detail as possible. Include any thoughts you had about possible negative outcomes.

Next, try to recall what actually happened. Write it down.

How accurate were your worries? Were your anxious thoughts useful as a coping strategy? Write down if your worries were useful or not.

Now that you've tried this exercise with something that happened in the past, try it with a situation coming up that you are worried about. Record all your anxious thoughts before the event and then record what actually happens. Again, you should ask yourself – how accurate were your worries? Were your anxious thoughts useful as a coping strategy?

Try not worrying!

One of the best ways to find out whether worrying is really helping is to stop and see what happens. Try the following experiment:

- For one day, keep worrying. Record what happens throughout the day. Also record how anxious you feel on a scale of 0 to 100 per cent.

- The next day, don't worry. Give yourself permission to let the worries go. Record what happens throughout the day. Also make a note of how anxious you feel on a scale of 0 to 100 per cent.

- Keep alternating days of 'worry' and 'no worry' for a week or two. Then compare your records for 'worry days' and 'no worry days'. Ask yourself: did worrying really help? How did worrying affect your anxiety levels?

If you try the exercises above, keep a record of the outcome. Use your findings to update the thought-challenging exercises you have been working on throughout this section of the book.

Challenging negative beliefs about worrying

We've talked about how believing that worrying is useful or serves some beneficial purpose can serve to keep the worry cycle going. But this isn't the only kind of belief about worrying that can be a problem. Some people believe almost exactly the opposite – that worrying is harmful to them in some way, or that it is uncontrollable. This can be thought of as 'worrying about worrying'. You may even find that you hold both kinds of beliefs about worrying – on one hand, you believe there is some benefit to worrying, but on the other hand you are worried about the fact that you can't seem to control or manage it, or that all that worrying is going to have a damaging effect on your health.

In this section, we will look at beliefs about the negative effects of worrying and how to deal with this problem.

Beliefs about the negative effects of worrying often fall into one of the following categories:

I'm worried because my worrying is 'out of control'

You may be plagued by thoughts such as, 'I can't stop worrying' or 'My worries are going to take over and control me'.

I'm worried that worrying is harmful

You may be thinking: 'I could go crazy with worrying' or 'It's not normal to worry' or 'If I keep worrying, I will have a nervous breakdown' or 'If I keep worrying, I'll have a heart attack'.

If you're afraid that your worrying is out of control or harmful, then you are likely to worry more, not less. This will make you feel more anxious, and you will therefore worry more – yet another vicious circle. Like other worries, these thoughts tend to be biased and based on exaggeration, and are not helpful.

If this is how you are feeling, read the following sections and try some of the practice exercises.

I'm worried because my worrying is 'out of control'

If you feel as if your worrying has completely 'taken over' your life, you may believe that there is very little you can do about it.

But let's consider this in a bit more detail. Think about what it's usually like when you are worried and anxious, then ask yourself the following questions:

- Do I eventually stop worrying?

- Can I think of times when something happened

(e.g. the phone rang) that interrupted or stopped the worry? What happened?

- Can I think of times when I did something (e.g. turned on the television or made a cup of tea) that interrupted or stopped the worry? What did I do?

- Have I ever succeeded in stopping myself worrying by distracting myself?

Now that you have thought more carefully about your worrying and your ability to stop worrying, it's a good time to note your conclusions. For instance, you may have realised that you don't actually worry all the time and that you are able to interrupt your worry sometimes. This shows that you have more control than you thought over your worrying. Look at your answers to the above questions and then ask yourself: 'What does this show about my control over worry?' Write your answer down.

The problem with trying to 'control' your thoughts

Most people would agree that as soon as you try not to think about something, you think about it even more! So a distressing thought becomes even more persistent and troubling.

You can prove this point by doing the following experiment:

For the next two minutes, do not think about a pink elephant. Do not let the thought or image of a pink elephant come into your mind.

What happened? Most people who try this experiment say they had difficulty not thinking about a pink elephant, or that an image of a pink elephant kept popping into their mind. It is extremely unusual for someone to say that they did not think of pink elephants at all.

So, what happens when you try not to think about a worry, or try not to think about something that might trigger a worry? Rather than helping you to not think about it, these attempts make it more likely that you will start worrying, or that you will continue to worry.

In other words, trying to force the worry out of your mind and just 'stop thinking about it' actually makes it pretty certain that you will worry.

Annoying though it is, the sad fact is that the more you try to stop thinking about something, the more you do think about it. And what's more, this will probably convince you (wrongly) that your worrying is indeed out of control. What you need is a strategy that is less likely to make the problem worse, such as controlled worry periods.

Controlled worry periods

To use controlled worry periods, follow these three simple steps:

- As soon as you notice that you are worrying, postpone it by telling yourself that you will allow time to worry about the problem later in the day.

- Choose a time in the day when you will give yourself fifteen minutes to worry (preferably not in the hour or two before bedtime).

- When this time arrives, allow yourself to worry for fifteen minutes and no more (set a timer if you need reminding!). Only spend the time worrying if you still feel it is necessary to worry. If the problem doesn't seem important any more, don't spend time worrying about it.

Postponing your worries is different from trying to suppress or ignore them. When you postpone a worry, you are not telling your mind to stop worrying. Instead, you are asking your mind to move the worry aside for a little while so you can focus on other things. Later, you will allow your mind to come back to the worry.

Use controlled worry periods for one week and see what happens. Then consider what you have found.

Write down in your notebook, or on a piece of paper, the heading 'Proof that Worrying Is Controllable', and list all your discoveries. This might include statements like: 'I am sometimes able to stop worrying', or 'When I keep busy, I don't worry nearly as much', or 'When I use controlled worry periods, I spend much less time worrying during the day'. You can use this list as a reminder in the future.

I'm worried that worrying is harmful

Many people who have long-term problems with anxiety are troubled by thoughts such as:

- 'It's not normal to worry – there must be something wrong with me.'

- 'Worrying may make me go mad or have a nervous breakdown.'

- 'Worrying may cause a heart attack.'

Thoughts like these make your anxiety even worse. It's very important to confront them so you can think more realistically about the effects of worrying.

Let's begin with concerns about whether worrying is normal or not.

It is not normal to worry – there must be something wrong with me.

Worrying is normal. Most people say that they worry, and, at some point in their lives, they find worrying distressing. In fact, it would be virtually impossible to find an adult who claimed that he or she never worried.

Do you find this hard to believe? If so, it might be a good idea to find out for yourself whether the people around you spend time worrying. Try the following experiment.

Ask four people – two people that you think may spend some time worrying, and two that you think don't worry at all (or don't worry very much) – whether they worry.

Have they ever worried 'too much' about something?

When was the last time they found themselves feeling worried about something?

Name	What they said about worrying
Joanne	She worries that her boss thinks she's not good at her job. She worries that she may be sacked. She sometimes worries that her boss knows she's worrying about her work performance. The last time she worried was this morning.

You may be surprised at what you discover! Think about the responses that people give you, and what this new information tells you about worrying being normal.

Based on this information, write down a fairer and more helpful description about how normal it is to worry in your notebook.

Keep reminding yourself about this, especially if you find the old concerns creeping back. Remember that changing the way you think about things takes time and practice but you can do it.

Worrying may make me go mad or have a nervous breakdown

Remember that almost everyone worries sometimes, and that most people say that worrying has, at some point, been distressing for them. Does this mean that most people have mental health problems? Of course not. Worrying is clearly normal and is not a sign of mental illness or breakdown.

Can worrying lead to a mental breakdown? The answer to this question is 'no'. It is true that it can make you feel tired and very unhappy, so you may feel as though you are about to crack up, but in fact this does not happen. The stress caused by worrying does not cause mental breakdown, either.

Our ancestors lived in conditions that were much more stressful than the conditions we face now. So if stress caused mental breakdown, humans would never have survived as a species.

Think about times in your own life when you were very worried and anxious. Perhaps you were taking your driving test, or had to give a speech at a large wedding. What happened? Did you have a mental breakdown? No.

Using these facts, write down in your notebook a more realistic thought about the effect of worrying on mental health.

Worrying may cause a heart attack

Can worrying cause a heart attack or damage your body in some other way?

The physical symptoms of anxiety can be quite uncomfortable and you may worry that anxiety is 'doing damage' to your body. However, remember that the physical symptoms are part of the fight-or-flight response (see pages 6–8) and are intended to activate our bodies for defence. This response is normal and healthy, if a bit uncomfortable.

Many of the physical symptoms experienced when we are anxious are very similar to those we have when we are exercising. This isn't surprising when you consider that the fight-or-flight response is really just your body preparing you for physical exertion. And we know that exercise is healthy and is even recommended by doctors!

Now write down in your notebook a more accurate comment about the effect of worrying on physical health.

Thinking about worrying in a more helpful way

Now read over everything you have written supporting the fact that worrying is normal and not harmful. Think about any proof for and against the belief that worrying is harmful. Based on this proof, you can sum up a more helpful way of thinking about worrying in a chart like the one opposite.

Now it's your turn. Copy these two column headings at the top of a new page in your notebook.

Underneath each heading, write down your original negative thoughts about the effects of worrying and then use your new knowledge to come up with some fairer and more helpful thoughts about the effects of worrying.

Negative thoughts about the effects of worrying	Fairer and more helpful thoughts about the effects of worrying
Worrying is not normal.	Worrying is normal – everyone worries sometimes.
Worrying may cause mental breakdown.	Worrying does not cause mental breakdown – it is a normal and is not harmful, even if it does feel horrible.
Worrying may cause a heart attack.	Worrying will not cause a heart attack. Feeling anxious is a normal and healthy part of being human. My heart may be pounding, but it also pounds during exercise.

You may need to repeat this exercise (and the exercises shown earlier in this section) whenever you find yourself 'worrying about worrying'. Remember that changing the way you think about things takes practice. Even if you don't quite believe what you are writing, put it down anyway. Some ideas take some getting used to, and you will find that the more you look at the new ideas, the more believable they will seem, and the less realistic the old ones appear.

Other strategies to help manage worrying

If we look at the kind of things people worry about, we see that people tend to worry about current problems or hypothetical situations that may occur at some point in the future. When you look at the thought records you completed (see page 40), what do you notice? Do you tend to worry about current problems in your life, or are you focused on problems that may occur sometime in the future? What you worry about can determine the best strategy to manage the worrying.

Problem-solving

If you are worried about current problems in your life, it can be useful to replace worrying with problem-solving. Problems that are occurring right now in your life can be dealt with by doing something, either to solve the problem or actively deal with its negative consequences. Often when people find themselves in the vicious circle of worrying and anxiety, they actually spend very little time deciding how they will solve problems. Instead, they get 'stuck', going over the same unhelpful thoughts over and over again. Making a specific and manageable problem-solving plan and then taking action can be very helpful in reducing anxiety.

Below is a list of the main steps in problem-solving that you may find useful.

The main steps in problem-solving

- **Define the problem.** Instead of just going over and over the problem in your head, try to be specific. Decide what exactly the problem is and, if possible, break it down into smaller problems.

- **Think about your resources and list possible solutions.** Have you ever solved a problem like this in the past? Do you have any personal strengths or knowledge that might help you solve this problem? Is there anyone who might be able to help you? After you've thought about these things, sit down with a pencil and paper and write down as many possible ways of solving the problem as you can think of. Don't worry if your ideas seem silly or unlikely to work – you are simply generating ideas.

- **Choose a solution.** Think about the pros and cons of each solution you have listed. Think about the likelihood of success, but also consider how much time and effort would be required and how much help you would need from others. Then decide on one solution that you will try to put into action. You don't have to choose a solution that will solve the problem completely, as long as it helps you move in the right direction.

- **Make a plan.** Break the solution down into small and manageable steps. Make each step very specific – it should be clear exactly what you need to do and in what order. If your plan is vague or unmanageable, it will be difficult to put it into action. For example, if your solution was 'I need to get a job', your steps to a solution might include 'Get a newspaper tomorrow and review the job advertisements', 'Update my CV on Tuesday morning' and 'Make at least one application by Friday'. Make sure you decide which steps you will work on first.

- **Do it.** Try out your solution, even if it is only the first step to solving the problem.

- **Review the outcome.** If your solution works, that's great. Congratulate yourself and remember this experience for the future. If your solution does not solve the problem, review what happened. Does your plan need to be reworked or do you need to try again? Remember that, even if you haven't yet solved the problem, you are at least facing up to it – and this is likely to help you solve it in the future.

Worry scripts

If you find yourself worried about hypothetical problems that may occur at some point in the future, problem-solving may be difficult. For example, no amount of problem-solving will address a worry that your child will be involved in a a car accident when he/she starts driving one day, or that your spouse may develop a serious illness later in life. When people worry about hypothetical problems in the future, they often focus on the worst possible outcome – but because the thought makes them so uncomfortable, they quickly push it out of their mind. As we discussed previously (remember the pink elephant?), this doesn't work very well, and usually results in the thought returning.

Interestingly, researchers have found that when people face these kinds of worries head on, the worrying tends to decrease. A good way to do this is to use a worry script. A worry script involves writing out all the details of the feared or worrying hypothetical problem situation, including everything you fear might happen and how you think you will feel. This is the opposite of avoiding worrying and the negative emotions that go along with it – rather, the process of writing out a worry script encourages you to face your fears, to think about what the outcome you fear really looks like, and experience the negative emotions that associated with it.

This may sound horrible, but researchers have found that if this process is repeated several times, anxiety and worrying start to decrease. If you stop pushing the worry away, it will stop creeping back in. Facing your fear also takes away its potency and allows you to opportunity to look at your worries objectively.

How to Write a Worry Script

- Set aside at least twenty minutes to complete a worry script.

- Decide what hypothetical worry you are going to focus on.

- Write out exactly what you are worried will happen. Imagine the worst-case scenario and what it would entail. Don't spare any details – describe all aspects of the feared outcome, including how you think you would feel and cope.

- If you feel anxious or upset while you are doing this – you are doing it right! Remember this exercise is designed to help you manage your anxiety and worrying over the long term. At first, this will be difficult.

- Repeat the exercise every day for two weeks. Each day, write a new worry script about the same worry.

- At the end of two weeks, notice how you feel when writing out your worry script. Do you feel as upset or anxious as the first time? What has happened to your day-to-day worrying about the same topic?

Some people worry that writing their worry down, or thinking about it in great detail, may make the worry come true. THINKING OR WRITING ABOUT SOMETHING DOES NOT MAKE IT COME TRUE. If it were true, thinking about what you would do if you won the lottery would mean that you were going to win the lottery.

5

Managing Anxiety by Changing Behaviour

Anxiety tends to have a significant impact on behaviour. Very often people do things to reduce
unpleasant anxious feelings, such as avoiding or
leaving situations that provoke anxiety, or engaging
in behaviours that make them feel a little bit safer
in these situations (such as occupying themselves
with their phone). Others do things to try to reduce
uncertainty in situations. All of these behaviours
have the same goal – to reduce anxiety. They may
provide some temporary relief, but in the long run
these actions only serve to keep the vicious circle
of anxiety going. If you really want to get anxiety
under control, it is important to take a careful look
at how your behaviour is contributing to the problem and then change it for the better.

Overcoming Avoidance and Safety Behaviours

Avoidance makes anxiety worse in the long run.

When you feel anxious, you usually want to get away from the difficult situation as quickly as possible or do something to make the situation safer. In a truly dangerous situation, this response would be quite sensible. You would escape, or protect yourselves from danger, and the anxiety response would gradually disappear. Similarly, it would probably be useful for you to avoid similar situations or use similar strategies to 'stay safe' in the future.

Problems start when we try to escape or avoid situations that aren't really dangerous. The more we do this, the more we reinforce the idea that there is something to be scared of. In the long term, this means that we become more and more scared of things. We never discover that the situation was not that bad, or that we could have coped with it.

Safety behaviours don't make you safe. It is natural to want to make a scary situation feel safer. This is why people tend to use 'safety behaviours'. For example, a person who finds that parties or other social events make them anxious might stay close to their friend or partner, or avoid saying very much, or drink a bit more than usual, or busy themselves helping out with food preparation.

Avoiding or escaping situations that trigger anxiety, or using safety behaviours to control anxiety, may make you feel better in the short term. But in the long term, the more you use these strategies, the more the fear grows, and the harder it becomes to face the situation. Each time you avoid or escape the situation or use safety behaviours, a negative message is sent. This message could be: 'The only reason nothing terrible happened is because I didn't do it', or 'I got out just in time', or 'The only reason I didn't put my foot in my mouth is because I stayed next to my wife and she did all the talking'.

Over time, the number of situations that cause anxiety tends to increase and it becomes more and more difficult to lead a 'normal' life. In order to reduce anxiety in the long term, it is important to break the pattern as soon as possible.

Identifying the problem

The first step is to work out whether you are avoiding or escaping particular situations and whether you are using safety behaviours. Ask yourself the following questions:

• What situations do I avoid because they make me anxious?

• Do I ever leave situations or activities because I feel anxious? If so, what kinds of situations?

- Do I have 'tricks' that I use to make me feel more comfortable in anxiety-provoking situations? If so, what tricks do I use?

To sum up, try making two lists:

1 Things that you have been avoiding, that you would like to start doing again

2 Safety behaviours that you have been using but want to get rid of.

Asking yourself 'why?'

Very often, people avoid or escape situations because they think something will go wrong. For example, someone who was avoiding attending a party might have thoughts like 'I might get into a state and embarrass myself' or 'What if I say something stupid and everyone laughs?'

Ask yourself: 'Why am I avoiding this situation? and What am I worried will happen?' and write down your answer in your notebook.

We usually use safety behaviours because we think that they will somehow prevent something from going wrong. For example, someone who thought, 'If I start talking I might say something wrong' might use the safety behaviour of not talking at a party. Or someone who thought, 'No one will want to talk to me and I'll end up standing alone in a corner' might decide to use the safety behaviour of sticking by their partner or friend.

Ask yourself: 'Why am I using this safety behaviour?' and 'What am I worried will happen if I don't use it?' and write down your answers.

Avoiding situations and using safety behaviours means that you don't get a chance to find out whether your fears are justified or not. But if you challenge yourself to face the situation and get rid of the safety behaviours, you can find out the truth – which is very often much better than you expect. This can help you think about things in a fairer and more realistic way and reduce anxiety in the long term.

Stopping your avoidance behaviours and reducing your safety behaviours

Now it's time to test your more realistic thoughts about your anxieties by doing the things you have been avoiding and by slowly reducing your safety behaviours. When you are planning to make these changes, consider the following tips:

• Don't worry if you feel anxious at first when you face a difficult situation – that is normal.

• Take things at your own pace. Start small and work up to the really 'scary' things that you have been avoiding.

• You don't have to get rid of all your safety behaviours in one go – take your time and drop them one by one. It might take a while, but it will make things easier if you take it slowly.

• Anxiety will not disappear immediately – it will take a little while. The longer you stay in the situation, the more likely it is that your anxiety will reduce.

• Don't expect all your anxiety to disappear as soon as you have faced a situation once or as soon as you drop a safety behaviour. If you've been avoiding that situation or using a particular safety behaviour for a while, it will probably take time and repeated efforts to get rid of the anxiety completely. The more you practise, the less anxious you'll feel.

Boost your confidence by keeping track of your progress – write down each thing you try and record the outcome. This means that when you do something you had previously been avoiding or get rid of a safety behaviour, you should pay attention to what happens. Did the thing you fear happen or did everything turn out all right? Here is an example.

What I did	What I was worried might happen	What actually happened
I went to a party.	I was worried that I would feel nervous and end up saying something stupid, or that I wouldn't have anything interesting to say.	I felt nervous, but it was nice to see my friends. I found I had some things to talk about. I felt more comfortable as the night went on.

I tried mingling.	I was worried that I would end up standing alone and people would wonder what I was doing, or that if someone spoke to me, I wouldn't be able to think of anything to say.	I was able to talk to a few other people and I didn't end up standing all alone. I was able to talk, even though my partner wasn't there to support me.
I spoke up in a meeting and commented on someone's proposal (I normally don't say anything!)	I was worried that no one would take any notice, or even worse, that everyone would look at me as if I was completely stupid.	The person doing the proposal looked a bit put out (maybe just surprised?) for a second but then said she thought I had a point.

On a new page of your notebook, copy down these column headings to make a chart for you to record your own behavioural changes, what you worried might happen, and the actual outcome.

Seeing things written down like this will help you think about things in a fair and realistic manner. But bear in mind that things might not always go well – that's life, and everyone has times when things don't quite go as planned! But just because something doesn't go well on one occasion, this doesn't mean it won't go well another time. Keep trying – this will help you develop confidence that you can manage situations, even when they don't go perfectly.

After you have tried a few things you had been avoiding, or dropped a few safety behaviours, it might be worth going back to the thought-challenging exercises on pages 41–8 and redoing them, using the new experiences you now have.

Overcoming your avoidance habits and getting rid of your safety behaviours will be hard work and will almost certainly make you feel anxious at times. You are, after all, changing habits that might have been with you for some considerable time, and which were intended to make you less anxious! So when you start to do things in a different way it is very likely that you will feel some anxiety, especially at first. It can take a lot of courage to stick with this anxiety. But remember: the anxiety is unpleasant but it won't harm you, and if you stick with this programme it will start to improve. So don't be discouraged! Reread the sections you feel helped you the most and redo some of the thought-challenging exercises. Take pride in what you have achieved so far.

Changing Behaviour to Increase Tolerance for Uncertainty

Often people who struggle with anxiety have a hard time dealing with situations in which they feel uncertain about the outcome. To help deal with this, they often engage in behaviours that they hope will reduce uncertainty, or avoid it completely. As we discussed in chapter 1, 'How Does Anxiety Affect Your Behaviour', some examples of this include:

• Reassurance seeking – repeatedly asking others whether they agree with you, or asking their opinion.

• Asking others to make decisions – avoiding the responsibility of making a decision in case it is the wrong one, even if it is about something very minor like what to have for dinner.

• Checking (and re-checking!) – this can involve behaviours like checking on others' safety or whereabouts (e.g. phoning or texting), or checking emails to make sure there is no 'bad news'.

• Excessive preparation – spending far too much time researching decisions or making to-do lists.

These strategies are similar in many ways to avoidance and safety behaviours. They are intended to reduce anxiety (by trying to avoid a feeling of uncertainty), and often involve avoiding uncertain situations altogether or engaging in behaviours intended to reduce feelings of uncertainty. These strategies do not work over the long run. If you really think about it – can you really avoid uncertainty? Probably not, unless you have a crystal ball! It is impossible to avoid uncertainty in life. Rather than trying avoid it (remember: avoidance tends to make anxiety worse in the long run), it can be much more helpful to learn to better tolerate it.

Much like many of the other strategies discussed in this book, the trick is to face it head on. In order to better tolerate uncertainty, you will need to put yourself in situations that make you feel uncertain (or stop using behaviours that make you feel more

certain when you find yourself in these situations –
this is just another form of a safety behaviour).

The first step is to think about whether you are
engaging in any behaviours such as reassurance
seeking, asking others to make decisions, checking,
or excessive preparation.

Write down any examples you can think of.

The next step is to purposely stop doing these things.
Are you not sure what pair of shoes to buy? Don't
ask for anyone else's opinion – force yourself to make
the decision on your own. Not sure what movie to
go to? Don't ask your friend to make the decision –
offer your opinion. Is your spouse five minutes late
coming home? Don't call his/her mobile to check
if they are OK. Spend excessive time making lists?
Force yourself to go to the store without one.

After you complete one of these tasks, write down
what you did in your notebook. Then write down
what happened. Did everything turn out OK?
If things went wrong, what did you do to cope?
Could you handle it? Remember, life is uncertain –
sometimes things will go wrong. But you might be
better able to cope than you thought.

6

Staying on Top of Things

Managing anxiety usually requires quite a lot of work. Practice is important. But the hard work will pay off. Progress may be slow, especially at first, so it's a good idea to keep track of how you are doing. For example, you may want to record a daily or weekly anxiety rating (from 0 to 100 per cent) or an estimate of time spent worrying, so that you can see improvement as time passes. If you notice successes, even small ones, congratulate yourself. Remember that your thoughts are very important. Telling yourself, 'I should have done it better' or 'Anyone could do that' is unhelpful. Encourage yourself, just as you would encourage someone else.

Everyone has good days and bad days. Some days your anxiety level will be high, and other days it will be low. A task that seems easy one day may feel difficult the next. Having a 'bad day' does not mean that you're not improving or that you will never get better. Setbacks should be expected. In fact, 'bad days' can be seen as good opportunities to practise your new techniques!

Anxiety is normal and it is unreasonable to expect a completely 'anxiety-free' life – everyone experiences anxiety from time to time, and everyone has periods when they worry too much. However, it is reasonable to try to manage anxiety more effectively and to be able to get on with life, coping with the 'ups and downs' as they come along.

Finally, it can be very useful to write down the most important things you have learned. You should also give some thought to any difficulties that you think may arise in the future and write down ideas for handling these problems. Below is a list of questions that you can use to help you keep track of your ideas. Keep your written work with this book, and refer back to it from time to time or whenever you start feeling anxious.

Summing up and preparing for the future

- What has been my most useful strategy to help manage my anxiety?

- Has anything else been helpful?

- Is there anything that I should make sure I keep doing in order to keep my anxiety levels at a manageable level?

- Looking into the future, are there any events or situations that might lead to me feeling anxious? If so, what are they?

- What should I do to help manage my anxiety in these situations?

- At times when my anxiety rises, what are the most important things to remember?

Other Things That Might Help

This book has provided you with an introduction to the problems of anxiety and what you can do to overcome them. Some people will find that this is all they need to do in order to see a big improvement, while others may feel that they need a bit more information and help. In that case there are some longer and more detailed self-help books around. Using self-help books, particularly those based on CBT, have been found to be particularly effective in the treatment of anxiety problems. Ask your GP if there's a Books on Prescription scheme running in your area – if there isn't, we recommend the following books:

Overcoming Anxiety by Helen Kennerley, published by Robinson

The Complete CBT Handbook for Anxiety, edited by Roz Shafran, Lee Brosan and Peter Cooper, published by Robinson

The Anxiety and Phobia Workbook by Edmund J. Bourne, published by New Harbinger Publications

How to Stop Worrying by Frank Tallis, published by Sheldon Press

Mind Over Mood by Dennis Greenberger and Christine A. Padesky, published by the Guilford Press

Sometimes the self-help approach works better if you have someone supporting you. Ask your GP if there's anyone at the surgery who would be able to work through your self-help book with you. Some surgeries have graduate mental health workers who would be able to help in this way, or who might offer general support. He or she is likely to be able to spend more time with you than your GP and may be able to offer follow-up appointments.

For some people a self-help approach may not be enough. If this is the case for you, don't despair – there are other kinds of help available.

Talk to your GP – make an appointment to talk through the different treatment options on offer to you. Your GP can refer you to an NHS therapist for cognitive behavioural therapy – most places now have CBT available on the NHS, although there can be a considerable waiting list. Don't be put off if you've not found working through a CBT-based self-help manual right for you – talking to a therapist can make a big difference. If an NHS therapist isn't available in your area or you'd prefer not to wait to see one, ask your GP to recommend a private therapist.

Although CBT is widely recommended for anxiety problems there are many other kinds of therapy available which you could also discuss with your GP.

Medication can be very helpful for some people and sometimes a combination of medication and psychological therapy can work wonders. However, you need to discuss this form of treatment and any possible side effects with your doctor to work out whether it's right for you.

The following organisations offer help and advice on anxiety problems and you may find them a useful source of information:

Anxiety Care UK
Email: recoveryinfo@anxietycare.org.uk
Website: www.anxietycare.org.uk

British Association for Behavioural and Cognitive Psychotherapies (BABCP)
Provides contact details for therapists in your area, both NHS and private.
Email: babcp@babcp.com
Website: www.babcp.org.uk

Mind
Tel: 0300 123 3393
Website: www.mind.org.uk

No Panic UK
Tel: 0844 967 4848
Email: admin@nopanic.org.uk
Website: www.nopanic.org.uk

An Introduction to Coping with Depression

2nd Edition

Lee Brosan and Brenda Hogan

ISBN: 978-1-47214-021-0

Overcoming app now available via iTunes and the Google Play Store

Practical support for how to overcome depression and low mood

Depression is the predominant mental health condition worldwide, affecting millions of people each year. But it can be treated effectively with cognitive behavioural therapy (CBT).

Written by experienced practitioners, this introductory book explains what depression is and how it makes you feel. It will help you to understand your symptoms and is ideal as an immediate coping strategy and as a preliminary to fuller therapy.

You will learn:
· How depression develops and what keeps it going
· How to spot and challenge thoughts that maintain your depression
· Problem solving and balanced thinking skills

Overcoming Anxiety

2nd Edition

Helen Kennerley

ISBN: 978-1-84901-878-4

Learn to master your anxiety using tried-and-tested techniques

We all know what anxiety feels like: it is an inevitable part of life. For some of us, however, panic attacks, phobias, obsessions or constant worries can have a devastating impact on our self-confidence, our relationships and our general well-being.

This self-help guide shows you how to uses cognitive behavioural therapy (CBT) techniques to manage your anxieties. CBT has been shown to be highly effective in the treatment of anxiety and it will help you to understand what has caused it, what is keeping it going and, crucially, how take back control.

This fully updated edition:
· Reflects recent developments in our understanding of anxiety
· Contains many useful examples of anxiety management in action

An Introduction to Coping with Extreme Emotions:

A Guide to Borderline or Emotionally Unstable Personality Disorder

2nd Edition

Lee Brosan and Amanda Spong

ISBN: 978-1-47213-732-6

Learn how to cope with extreme or unstable emotions

Many people suffer from extreme emotions with around 2% of people being diagnosed with Borderline Personality Disorder. It is a very troubling condition which causes abnormal and unstable behaviour including overwhelming feelings of distress and anger, which may lead to self-harming, damage or destruction of relationships and, at times, loss of contact with reality. Through clinically proven dialectical behaviour therapy (DBT) techniques, this book will help you to control your extreme emotions.

You will learn:
· The symptoms of personality disorder
· Different ways of coping with overwhelming emotions
· How to increase your emotional resilience from day to day

The Complete CBT Guide for Anxiety

Roz Shafran, Lee Brosan, Peter Cooper

The Complete
CBT Guide for
Anxiety

A self-help guide for anxiety, panic,
social anxiety, phobias, health anxiety
and obsessive compulsive disorder

An OVERCOMING publication

EDITED BY
ROZ SHAFRAN, LEE BROSAN AND PETER COOPER

ISBN: 978-1-84901-896-8

Overcoming app now available via ITunes and the Google Play Store

A highly respectable and authoritative self-help guide on all the anxiety disorders: generalised anxiety disorder, health anxiety, panic, phobias, social anxiety, OCD.

Edited by three leading CBT clinicians in the UK, this comprehensive guide offers individual CBT-based treatments for a wide range of anxiety problems. Each individual treatment reflects current the treatment in the UK for that anxiety disorder and is written by the clinician responsible for developing that treatment in the first place.

An ideal resource not only for those experiencing anxiety problems, but CBT therapists and IAPT workers.